KIDS BOOK OF NUMBER GAMES 1-70 WORKBOOK

All Rights reserved. No part of this book may be reproduced or used in any way or form or by any means whether electronic or mechanical, this means that you cannot record or photocopy any material ideas or tips that are provided in this book.

Copyright 2016

Exercise your brain and enjoy the different Number activities!

COLORING BY NUMBERS

Color the pictures according to the color of the numbers.

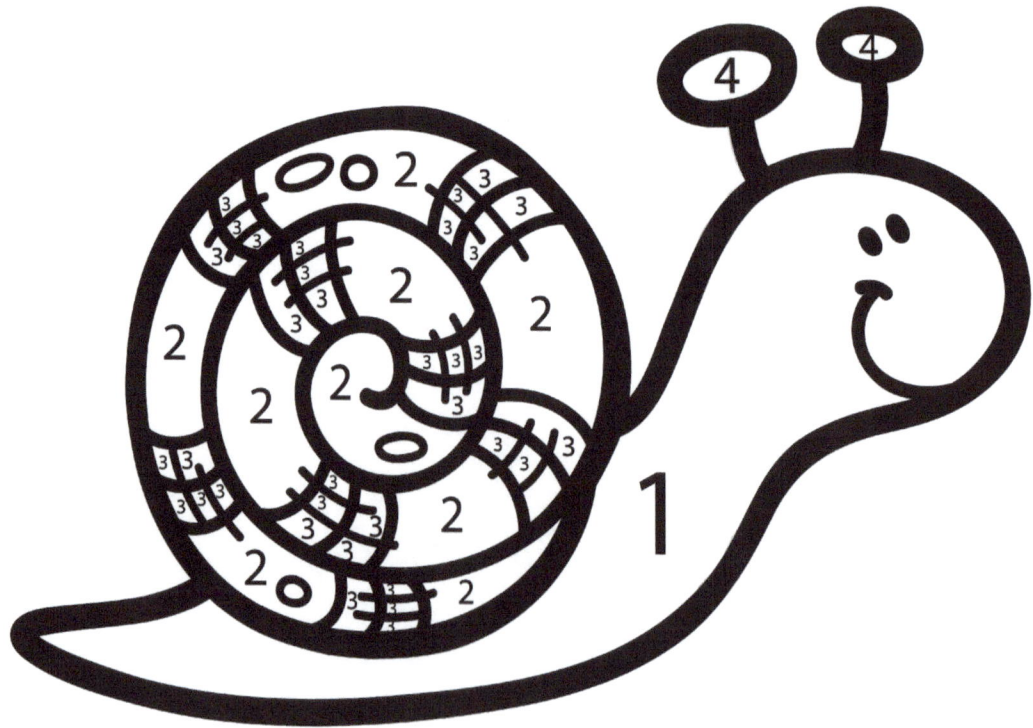

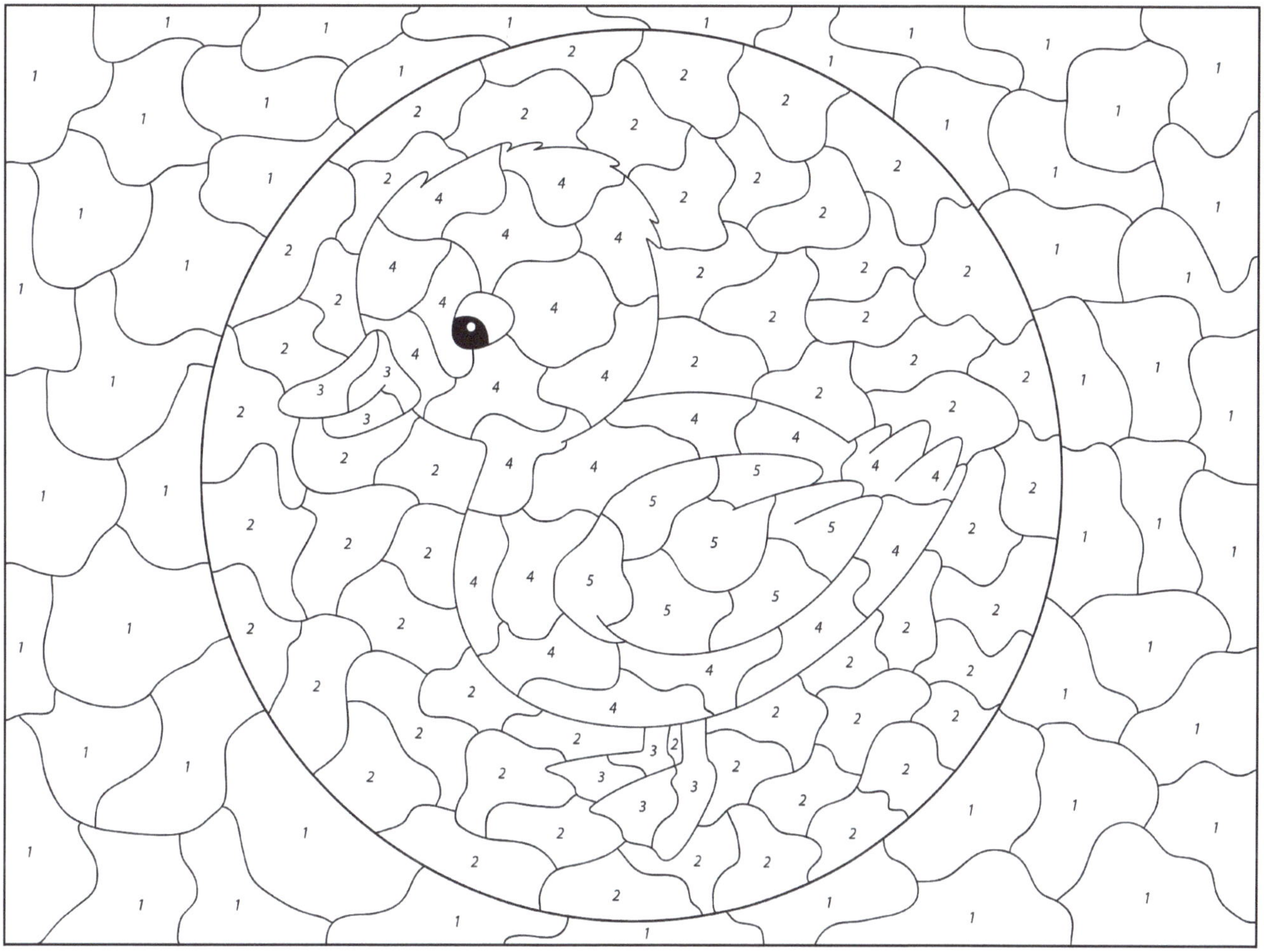

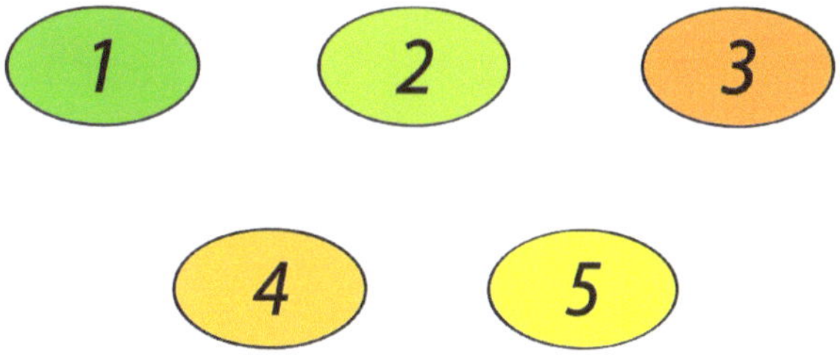

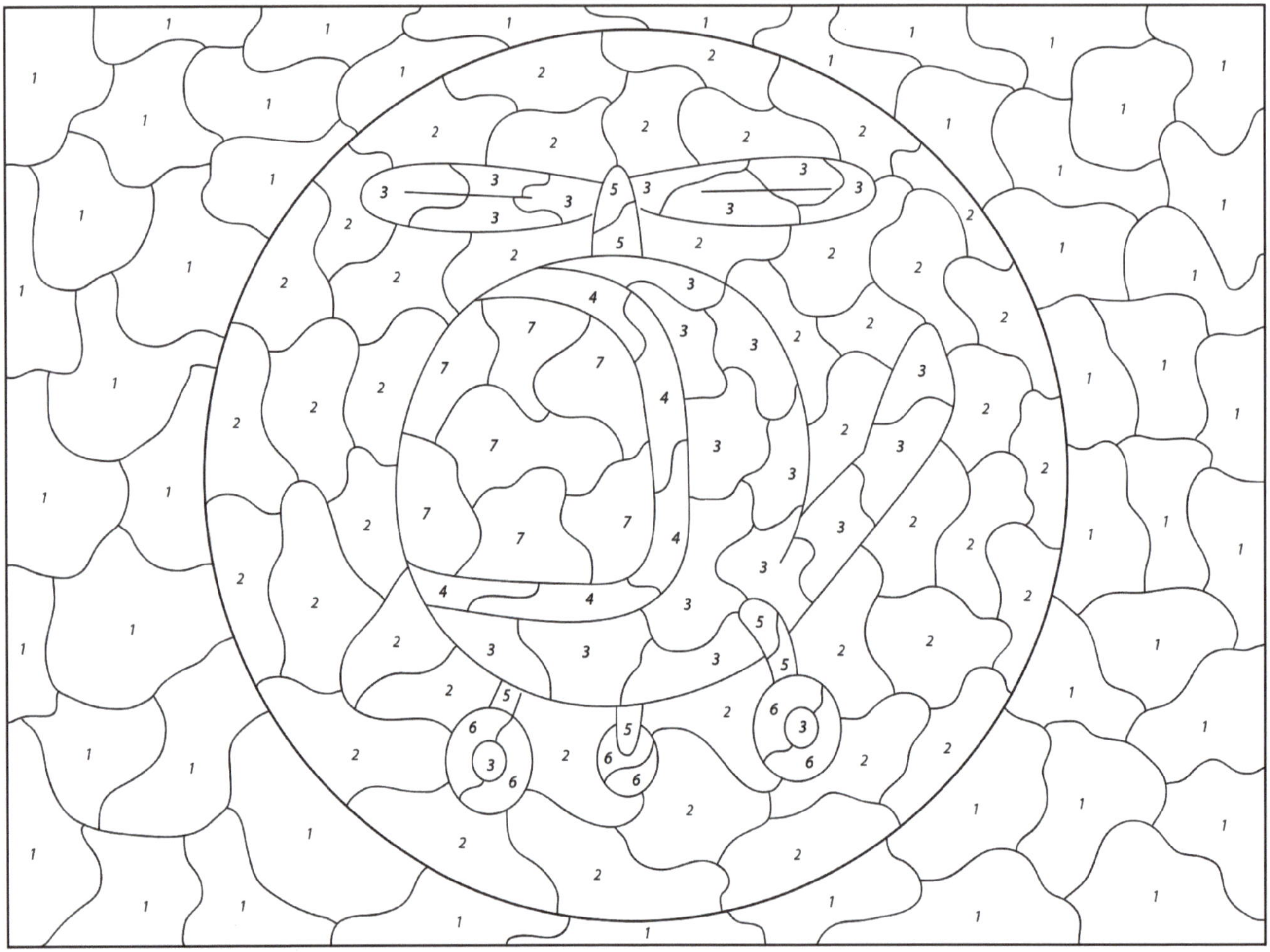

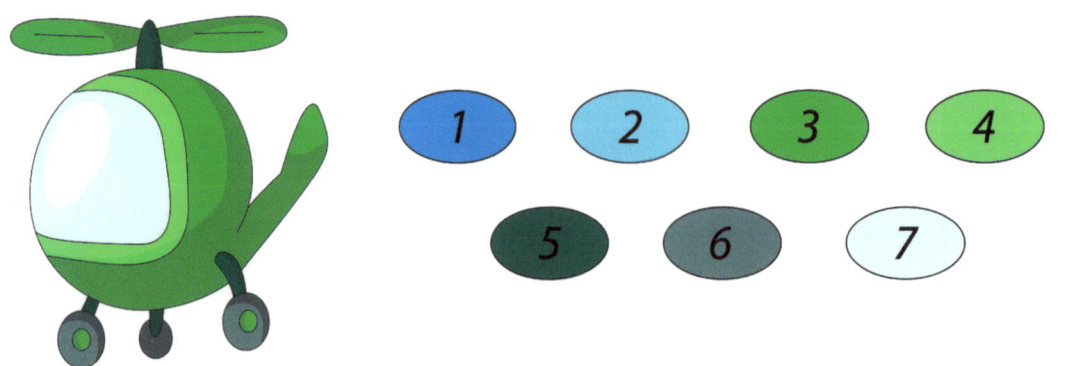

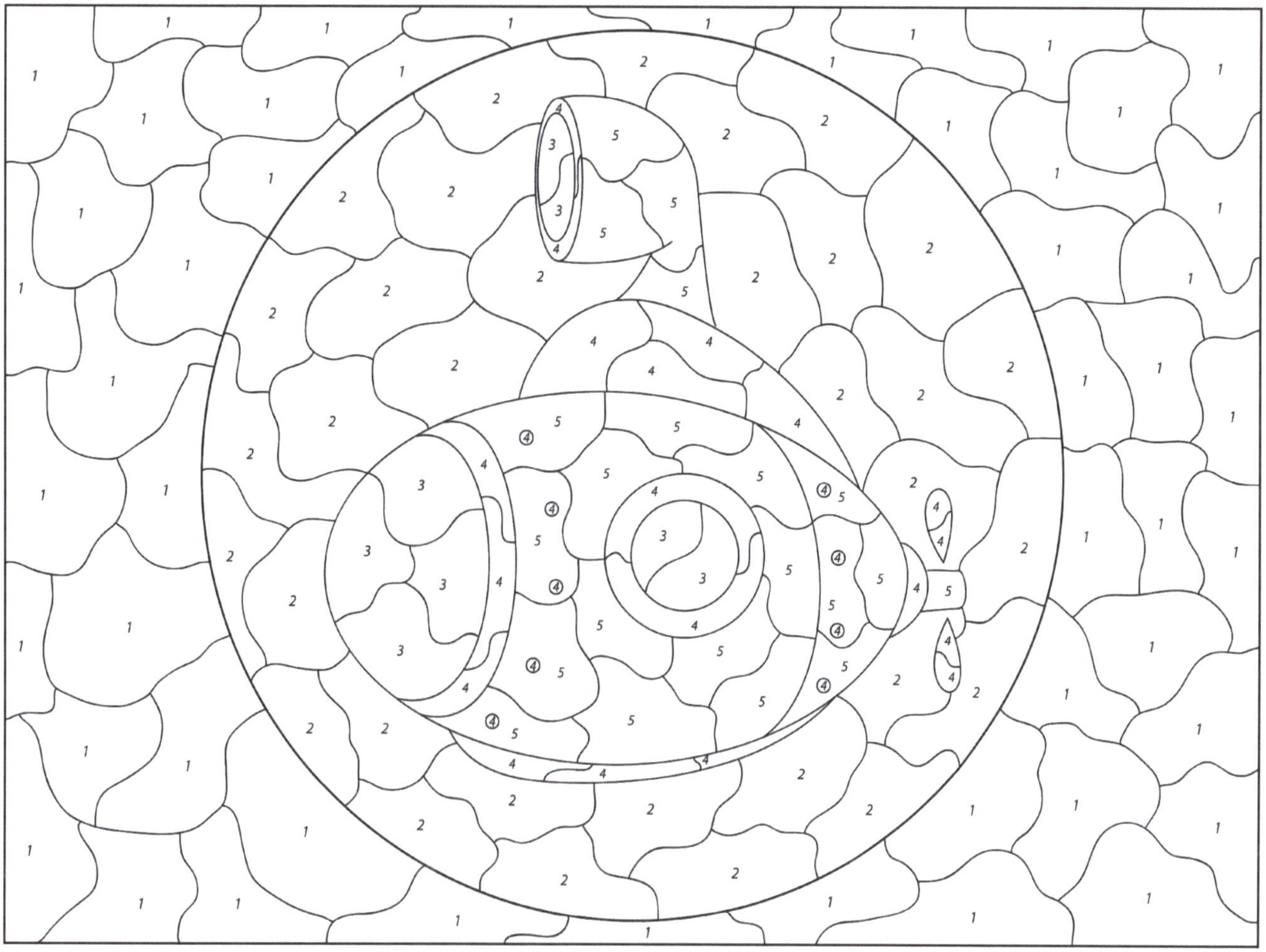

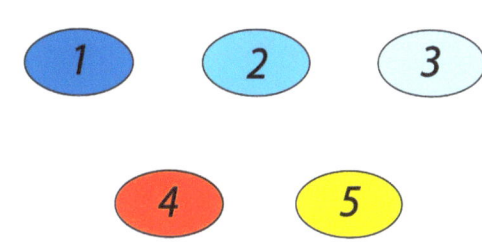

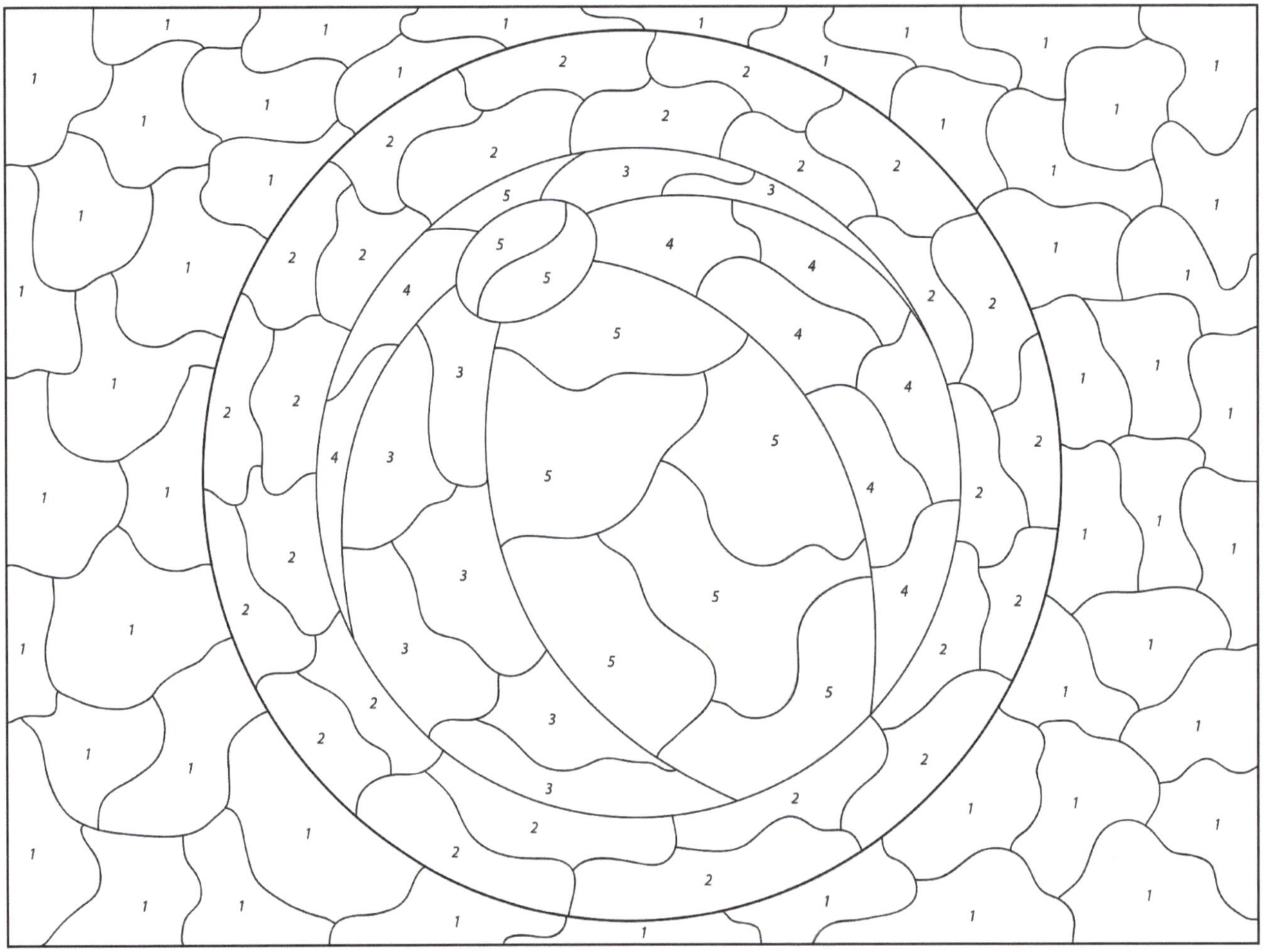

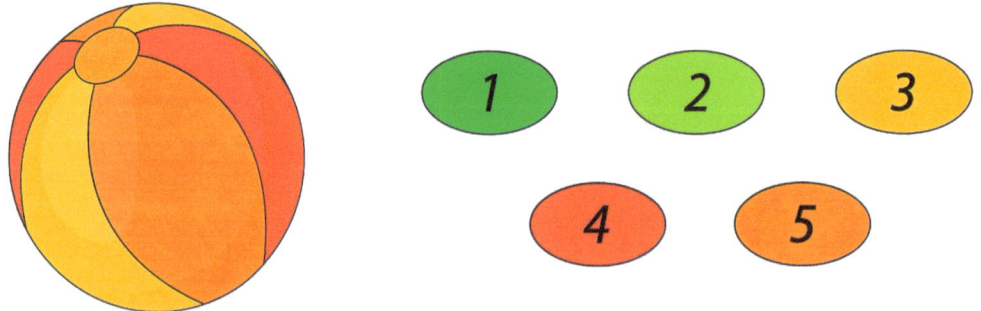

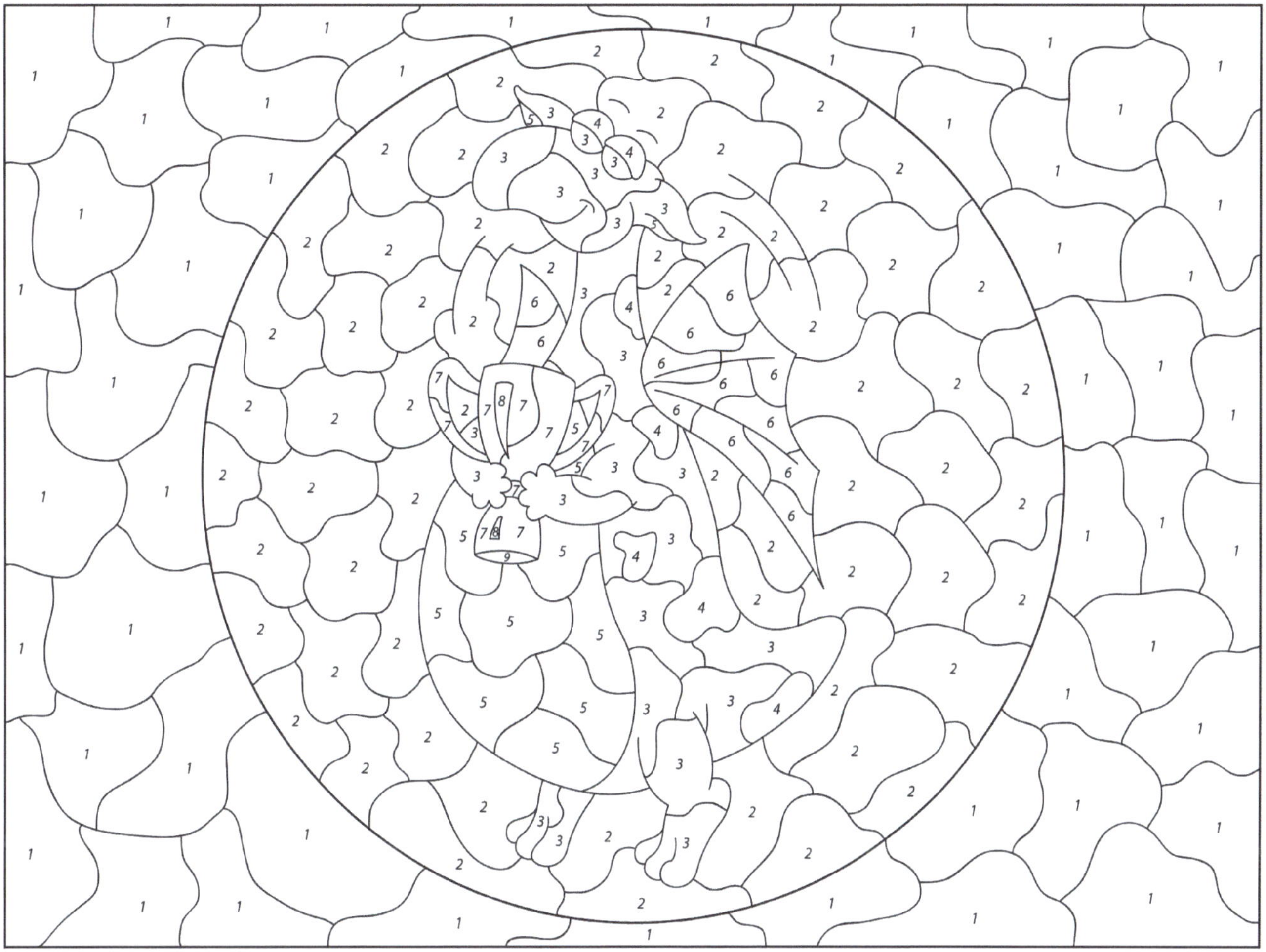

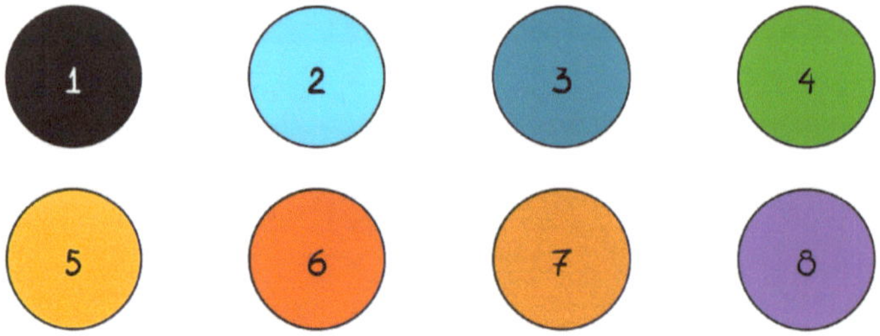

CONNECT THE NUMBERS

Connect the numbers to complete the drawings.

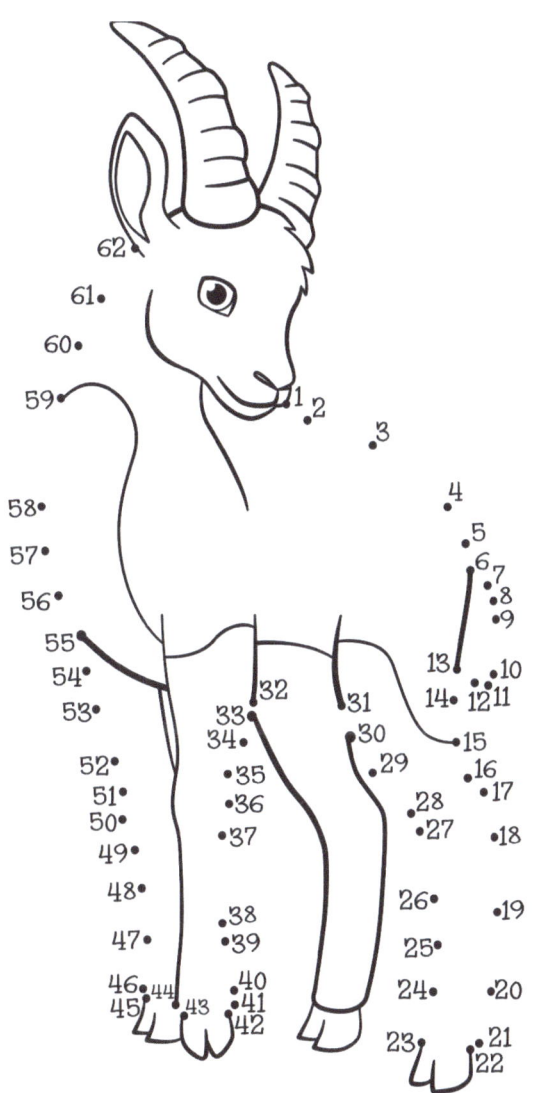

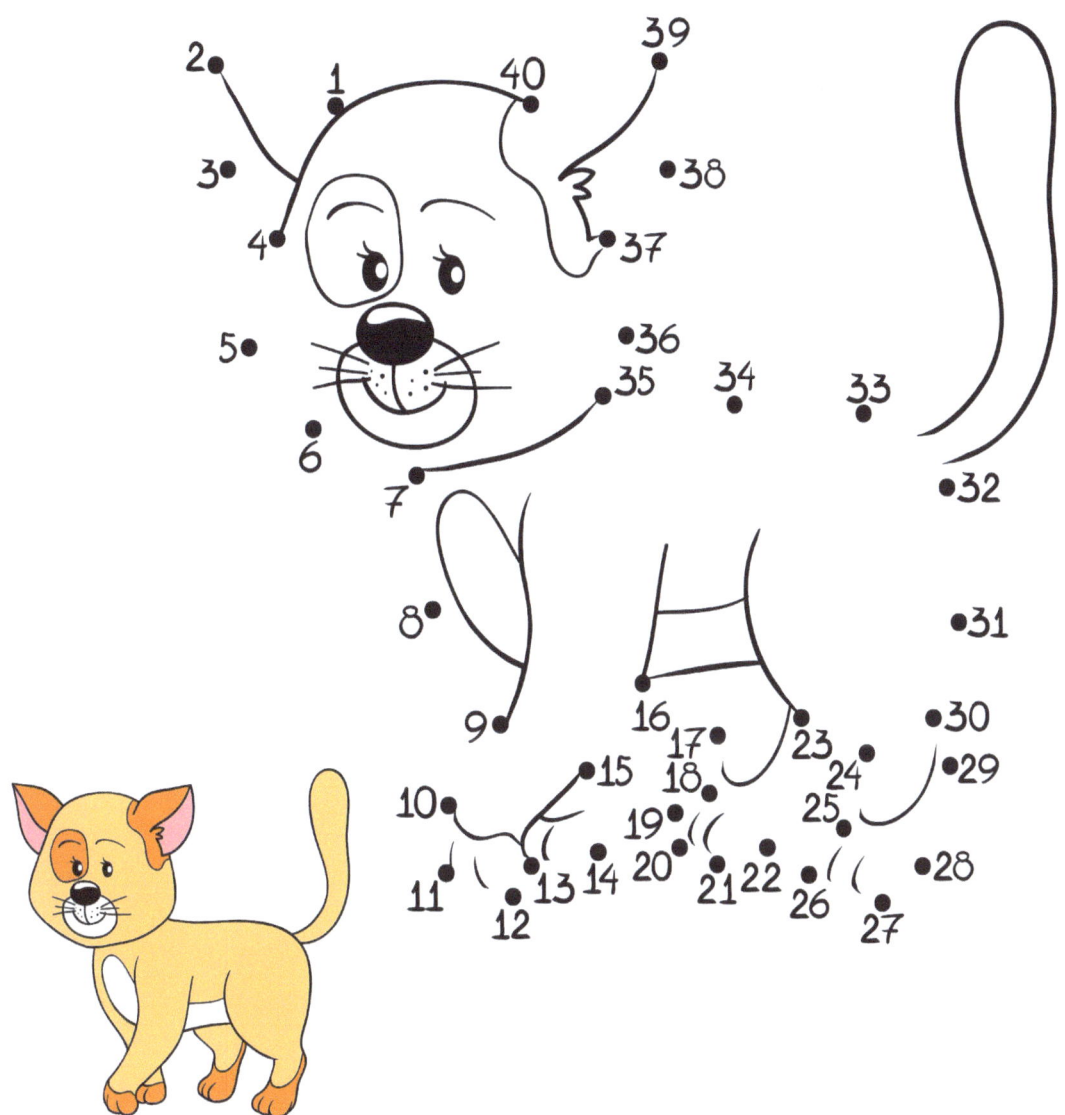

LET'S COUNT THE NUMBERS

HOW MANY DOGS DO YOU SEE?

2

HOW MANY PIGS DO YOU SEE?

3

HOW MANY
FISH
DO YOU SEE?

HOW MANY MICE DO YOU SEE?

5

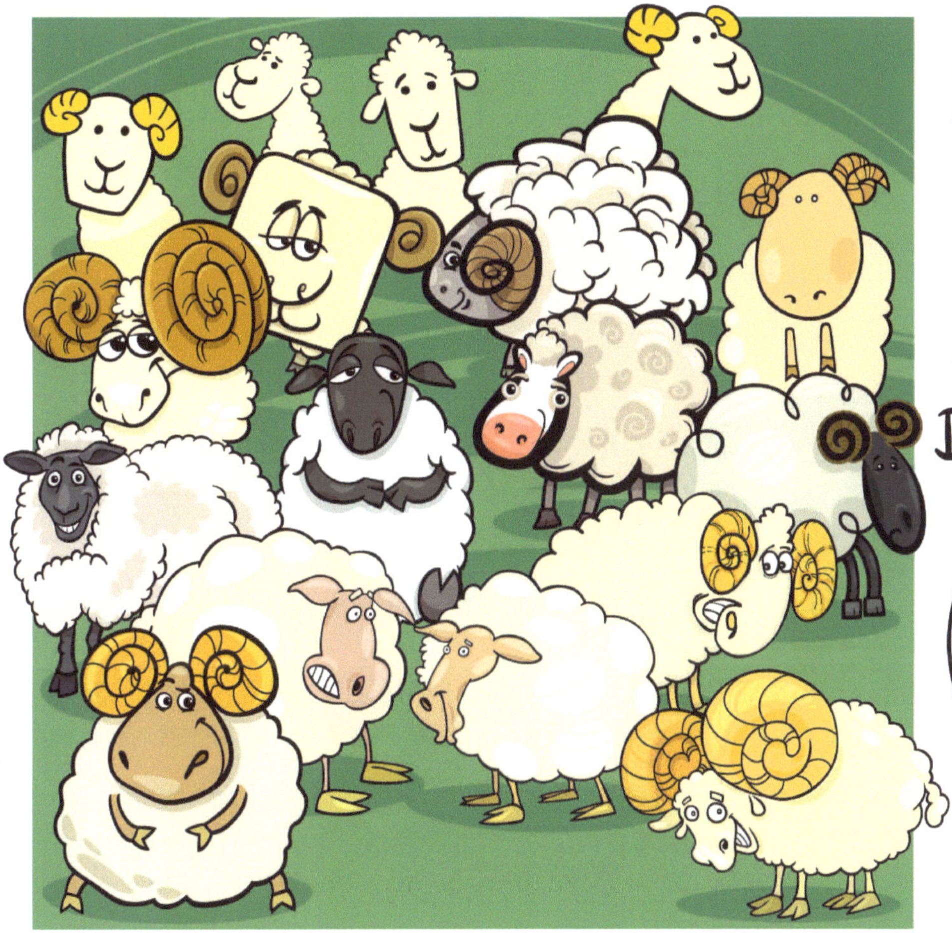

HOW MANY SHEEP DO YOU SEE?

?

6

HOW MANY **BEARS** DO YOU SEE?

?

7

HOW MANY BUNNIES DO YOU SEE?

9

HOW MANY
ELEPHANTS
DO YOU SEE?

10

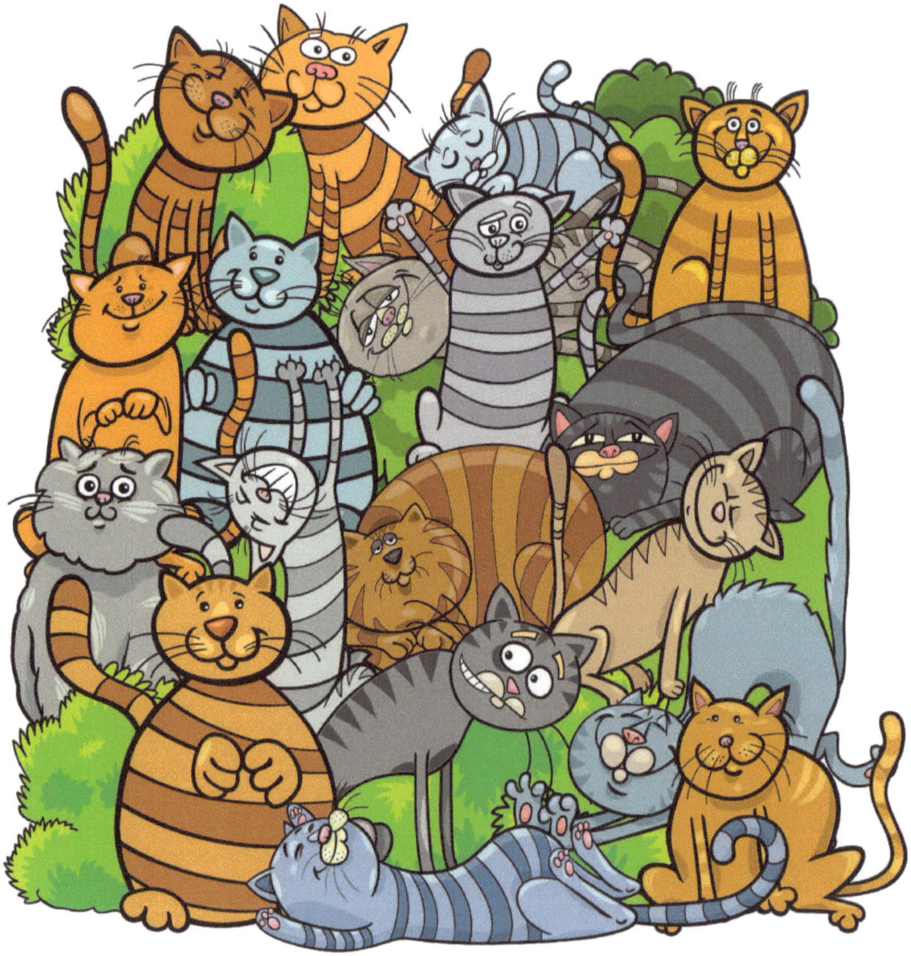

HOW MANY CATS DO YOU SEE?

?

Answers for "LET'S COUNT THE NUMBERS"

1. 19
2. 13
3. 11
4. 15
5. 17
6. 16
7. 21
8. 15
9. 10
10. 18

www.ingramcontent.com/pod-product-compliance
Lightning Source LLC
Chambersburg PA
CBHW041225040426
42444CB00002B/51